A bath for a calf

These mothers all have babies.
You have probably heard that
a baby cow is called a calf.
But each of these other babies
is a calf too.

Moose

Whale

Elephant

Hippo

Many of the babies' fathers do not help look after them. If the father can't do half the work, the mother must look after the calf by herself. Sometimes a grandmother helps too.

This calf enjoys basking in the afternoon sun.

This calf swims across a river with his mother.

This calf covers her skin in mud to keep cool.

This calf would rather take a cool bath.

This calf thinks baths are fun, so she runs fast to take a bath with her mother. At last she is in the calm water. Her mother helps her get clean.

This calf is always in a bath!
His home is the vast sea.

This calf is in a class of his own. He can swim fast.

This calf never has to take a bath. She has oil in her skin. She would rather eat green plants.

One day, she will reach
food high in the tree.

This is another calf that never needs a bath. He would rather eat grass.

Words to blend

bath	after	can't
basking	afternoon	rather
grass	fast	vast
class	plants	last
calf	calm	half
fathers	probably	always

A bath for a calf

Before reading

Synopsis: It's not just a baby cow that is called a calf. This book explores other babies called calves and some of the things they do.

Review phonemes and graphemes: /ear/ ere, eer; /air/ are, ear, ere; /j/ ge, dge, g; /s/ c, ce, sc, se, st; /c/ ch; /u/ o, o-e, ou; /e/ ea; /r/ wr

Focus phoneme: /ar/ **Focus graphemes:** a, al

Book discussion: Look at the cover, and read the title together. Ask: *Do you know what a calf is?* Allow children to share their ideas. Then ask: *What kind of book do you think this will be? How do you know? What do you think we might learn in this book? Why?*

Link to prior learning: Remind children that the sound /ar/ as in 'far' can also be spelled 'a' and 'al'. Turn to page 4 and ask children to find at least one word with each spelling of the /ar/ sound (calf, half, father, fathers, can't).

Vocabulary check: vast: very big or huge – 'the vast sea' is the author telling us that the sea is very big!

Decoding practice: Display the words 'calf', 'grass', 'plants' and 'calm'. Can children circle the letter string that makes the /ar/ sound, and read each word?

Tricky word practice: Display the word 'many'. Challenge children to circle the tricky part of the word ('a' which makes the /e/ sound). Practise reading and writing this word.

After reading

Apply learning: Discuss the book. Ask: *What did you think about the book? What was the most interesting thing you learned from reading it? Which animal was your favourite?*

Comprehension

- What is a baby moose called? (a calf)
- Why doesn't the calf on page 12 need to take a bath? (because he lives in the sea)
- How does the calf on page 8 keep cool? (by covering her skin in mud)

Fluency

- Pick a page that most of the group read quite easily. Ask them to reread it with pace and expression. Model how to do this if necessary.
- Challenge children to read page 10 with lots of expression, as if they were a TV presenter.
- Practise reading the words on page 17.

Tricky words review

have	many	of
the	do	one
to	are	two
because	people	was
once	friend	water